GOODBYE MOON,
HELLO SUNSHINE!

GOODBYE MOON, HELLO SUNSHINE!

SUNSHINE HUNTIN

CONTENTS

This book is dedicated to anyone suffering from grief, depression, anxiety, or any form of mental-related disorders, including PTSD. Or for those individuals who have felt bullied, rejected, abandoned, ghosted, betrayed, lost, stuck or terrified or simply recovering from a traumatic event. If you're afraid of being alone or failing at life?

Then may this collection bring you comfort in knowing that this is the human experience. May it give you strength in those dark moments to forge ahead and fight your way through, to find the moments of ease and peace that become your new normal. May these difficult feelings you experience be messages or road signs leading you in a new direction. Carving out a shiny new path for a brighter future.

FOREWORD

Many clouds come into our lives each day. Some stay and cause long spells of rainy days and stormy nights. While others bring fluffy cotton candy puffs of clarity to an afternoon delight. Then every once in a while, we are faced with a force so strong it clears away the life we labored on for so long. Breaking it apart piece by piece, sending it all into the wind until there is nothing left but you and your memories left to live in.

I don't know what possesses a person to treat others so terribly when all we truly want as humans is to be loved? To be accepted. To feel worthy. I'm talking about those individuals that aim to destroy other human beings. Out of greed, power, jealousy and rage. Those everyday bullies we encounter. creating chaos and fear wherever they wander. When they send you stormy days of destruction, you still shine your sunlight and hope to watch the miracles appear.

Have you ever thanked someone for the pain they inflicted upon you? I know that seems very saintly. The way I see it, we have three choices; we can be enraged in anger for what they did to us. Or lay on the floor crying like a victim. These options are not going to solve anything. We could take their jealousy, anger and resentment and turn it into a gift.

What was aimed to destroy our lives and create chaos, we could use to restructure and build a better life. A life of our dreams. When they tried to instill fear and terror, we could decide to grow stronger and more stable. No, not every time are we going to be successful in accomplishing this momentum, but it's a start. A jumping-off point into a new way to fight back against all that negativity. See if we could look at every moment of destruction, chaos and hate not as the tornado as it appears but as a gift. Not because they weren't devastatingly painful. Absolutely not. Small victories we used to navigate and find new ways to survive. And eventually we will grow despite their hatred and negativity. Not by force. By making a conscious choice, to adapt. Find a solution, despite the pain and betrayal they caused. They will see that we can actually thrive in the wake of their destruction. Realize that NOTHING will shake us, like the ancient oak, we stand protected and strong, shining our light like a beacon into the night.

When the world takes what seems like everything from you and there is no safe harbor from a storm. Will you create a blessing or only see a curse?

A COLLECTION OF POETRY BY

Sunshine Huntin

Chapter one, Goodbye Moon

Mr. Moon

darkness

my sweet darling dear

meet me at midnight

as the harvest moon

waves

the full moon

the moon dances

there you are...

the bee's knees

i feel your call

my sleepy moon

moments in time

snapped awake

morning moon

oh crescent moon

surrender

goodbye moon,hello sunshine!

Chapter Two, Hello Sunshine!

Be the sun

thoughtless whispers

deep thaw

rise

build a dam

i am right there

sunsets

oh sunbeam

silhouette

it's time

blinded

speak your truth

a blessing

the darkness

think of me

the light of my soul

my sunshine

my love

velvet mist

desert

i want to feel beautiful

inner light

intoxicated kiss

imagine if...

you are my sunshine

my sweet sunshine

i long

the sweet smell

what have you done?

❧ I ❧
GOODBYE MOON

MR. MOON

i stay up late
and wait
Mr. Moon knocks upon my single window pane
when fears arise about my fate
he shows his lusty face
as if to say…
"it's time to take a stand
there's a new life waiting
just for you
in some far-off distant land"

darkness
i will
no longer fear you
protected
i stand before you
bestow your wisdom
upon my soul
allow me to see
all the light
that shines within me

my sweet darling dear
i close my eyes
and dream
of how
i'd wrap my arms
around you
like a shroud of love
from the stars above
to stop the lies quite my mind think of how
to find
a way
to dream on a day
without
fear
to whisper in your ear how soon this distance
will disappear
so you can feel me near

meet me at midnight
underneath
the full
moonlight
magnetic memories
of your sweet kiss
fill my fevered dreams
with pure bliss

as the harvest moon
hangs low
determination
creeps upon my soul
my muse of magnetic motion
fills me with the most delightful potion

❧ 2 ❧
WAVES

waves rush, gush, and swirl
around my toes
i walk in
a little farther
a blanket of water rolls
across my skin
cleansing all that
lies within
the moon beckons
the tide away
only to bring
another rushing
my way

the full moon

is shining bright
in my window
tonight
i can't help
but make a wish on this bright, white
satellite
its magnetic wonder
pulls me in
holds me tight
keeps me safe
on this crisp
winters evening night

the moon dances
overhead
in the morning sky
while the sun
rest
in a deep slumber
beyond
the mountain ridge
the fall air
is cool clean
but dense with moisture
it's the kind of air

that fills your soul
and makes it sing

there you are....
with that
Cheshire cat grin
as you perch upon
the morning sky
beckoning me
to choose my path
to set myself free
just surrender
to this beautiful madness
that lies
within me

3

"THE BEE'S KNEES"

it's time to dream on a moonbeam
to make a wish
on a fancy dish
to smell the ocean breeze
to take a float
on "the bee's knees"
to feel the world
ALL around me
to coast along
listening to our
favorite song
to make a toast
on the things
we cherish the most
to feel you near
even when you are
not here
to close my eyes
and sing a dream
of what my future
just might bring

i feel your call
like a silent beacon
in the night
pulling me
towards you
like a magnet
i can't look back
i have tasted
the sweet abyss
of freedom
the call
of a new adventure

4

MY SLEEPY MOON

i pause to inhale
the blanket
of blue sky
when i noticed you
my sleepy moon
you stayed awake just to bid me adieu

moments in time
feel priceless
as i sip
a glass of wine
while the clouds
slow dance
across
the night sky

snapped awake
by wild thoughts of you
that beckon from my soul
as i dangle
in your
delicately woven web
where the wind begins to stir
an echo stops its call
the ocean meets the sand
and the moon begins to glow
suddenly every moment
starts to flow

❈ 5 ❈

MORNING MOON

i close my tired eyes as the morning air
washes away my slumber
i hear the song birds
cascade
across the sky
i look to the heavens
there you are
my sweet morning moon
to wish me good day
and a promise
to see me soon

oh crescent moon
nestled neatly
in the evening sky
you smiled
upon my soul today
and let my worries
fade far,
far away

6

SURRENDER

as i gaze upon a coal-colored sky
the moon greets me with his devilish grin
like a
iconic battle commander
aching for a battle cry
he hides away
his darkest sins
i notice the stars seem whiter and brighter and sparkle a
bit more
i can't help
but delight
in their splendor tonight
as an arrow stream
of shooting stars
is set sail upon my flesh
there is no place for me
to run
no place for me to hide
for i shall
make a wish
to remember

that soon the sun
will also rise
i might as well surrender
take it all with pride

7

GOODBYE MOON, HELLO SUNSHINE!

i kissed
the moon,
GOODBYE
and held close
the way
we used to be
forgave myself
for failing to see
the shadows you were reflecting back to me
i kissed the sun,
HELLO
and reflect in quiet gratitude for all the lessons
that you gave to me
then i choose myself today and let the rest ALL fade away

II
HELLO SUNSHINE!

be the sun on a rainy day
be the moon
on a cold dark night
be the stars
that surround us
with love and light
cus you are a gift
so please, please
treat yourself right

thoughtless whispers
of pain
set me free
to love
each part of me
so i can pry open
the cage doors
release my spirit
to fly free
light my fuse ablaze
into the autumn breeze

❧ *9* ❧

DEEP THAW

as my blue tinged fingers
reach behind
the frozen peas and tater tots
i remember...
where i placed you
for safekeeping
now you're covered
in ice crystals
with freezer-burnt edges
forgotten damaged
some would say
broken beyond repair
but there is
deep love
tucked inside
that double zip-locked bag
only one thing
will set this
frozen heart free
the sun and me

❧ 10 ❧

RISE

i finally said
ENOUGH
is ENOUGH
so this is
my trumpet call
this is
my BATTLE CRY
how dare you take from me
the sun that shined so bright within me
i might be bruised and broken
but i shall forge ahead
stronger
from sheer
strength of will
i lift my
shield
draw my sword
and swiftly remove you
from the path ahead
you can trust
that I WILL RISE
AGAIN!

BUILD A DAM

as the
sunlight
peers
through
the stormy thoughts
of my soul
i build a dam
by will and strength
to hold back
the tears
that spill
down my face
for i will rise
once more

i am right there
with you
set fire to your pain
burn away
those dark thoughts
and walk
amongst the flames

SUNSETS

the most magnificent
sunsets of my life
fell amongst the landscape
of cloudy skies
and days upon days
when my soul
howled
for a reprieve
from the pain
it survived

oh sunbeam
as you flicker
through the leaves
like a shooting star stream
you heal my scars
without a single trace
from a solidarity
embrace

❧ 13 ☙

SILHOUETTE

**i crave your
silhouette
in the sunset**

it's time\
to go\
outside\
feel the sun\
on my puffy eyes\
soothe my soul\
take a different pace\
reach my arms out wide\
to burn away\
this old hide\
to see what's been\
lurking below\
this forgotten place\
we all know

blinded
by the dense weight
of dust and smoke
fill the air
my heart beats
steady
flames stab
as they fortify
and encircle me
my world burns
down around me
finally, i am free
oh, how i have
waited
for this day
to be

speak your truth
set me free
i will let you
see
the real me
never assume
in betrayal and doom
believe in
our soul's light truth
i am right there
with you
set fire
to your pain
burn away
those dark thoughts
and walk amongst
the flame

**a blessing
a gift
a much-awaited
sigh of relief
so tears of joy
fall upon
my rosy cheeks
as kindness strikes
away my grief**

the darkness
drifts away
as the
sunlight
heals
the pain

think of me...
under the winters rain
may the starlight
heal your pain
tell me all
your secret pleasures,
mi amor
so the sun
can rise and shine
once more

the light of my soul
peaks
over the
canyon ridge
nestled
amongst the
clay earth
i begin
with a deep inhale
a fiery tornado
smolders
within my skin
with a slow and gentle flow
i let my fury go
into the wind

my sunshine,
thank you for making
all my clouds
go away
so i can smell
the nectar
of orange blossoms
blooming
that sweet way
for taking the time
to send me
some warmth today
what kind of girl
would I be?
if i didn't
take the time to say
"Merci Beaucoup"
for making my
gray skies turn blue

my love
with the
same dedication
as the sun
i will
search for you
the way
the sunlight
tracks the
morning mist

❧ 14 ❧
VELVET MIST

beauty
carves
through
layers of
shadows
creating
a velvet mist
of untamed vines
have no fear
your sunshine
is almost here
soon
your path
will be clear

15

DESERT

I crave you like
the sunbaked desert
craves the rain

I want to feel beautiful
to look
at my reflection
and like
the person looking
back at me
I want to walk
on the beach
and be free to just be me
I want to sing
and dance and
throw a party till three
most of all
I want to live the life
that was meant for me

16

INNER LIGHT

Written on March 17, 2021, St. Patrick's Day, Los Angeles, CA

we fill our lives
with pots of gold shows
and rainbows
we slurp and burp
and drink it down
with lots of fun
then return
to fill our goblets
with the magnetic rays
of the sun
as we dance and laugh our way
into the night
may we never forget to share
our inner light

intoxicated kiss
i remember you
so electrifying!
with a fevered passion
that has smoldered
for a thousand lifetimes
you are my beacon
in the darkest
of ocean tides

imagine if...
i kissed
your cheek
your lips
your nose
and even the
tips of your toes
i'll twist my fingers
through your
salt and pepper hair
i just can't help
but stare
your energy your beauty
has always been
right there
i just failed
to see
you were walking
right next to me

**you are my
sunshine
on a cloudy day
my inspiration
when everything
falls away
my beautiful,
sweet nectar
my treasure
that I promise
to love forever**

my sweet sunshine
you never stop
you never go away
no matter how
far apart we stay
even on the grayest days
your beams of light
shine away
warming
my heart and soul
each day

i long
to have your fingertips
upon my thighs
to feel the weight
of your body
against mine
to touch your face
to feel the sting
of your kiss
as you bite
my lips
to see the blue sunrise
of your soul
in the vast ocean
that lies between us
as the tides rise
and fall
you have given me
the world
as i long
for the sound
of your sweet call

the sweet smell
of longing fills the air
the iridescent clouds
drift across the sky
like a bowl
of cotton candy
with an aroma
so thick
i can taste
the sugar on my lips

what have you done?
my heart feels full
and warm like the sun
it makes me want to grab your hands
hold them tight
and love you
with all my might.
oh, how you make my heart swoon.
i think i just leaped
over the moon!
makes me want to grab your cheeks
kiss your lips and run around
a grassy meadow
while i do back flips
to laugh and dance
giggle and prance
to take a chance
to finally enjoy
a proper romance
oh my sweet, sweet love
you're my greatest wish from above
i know we'll make it a blast
and have so much fun
enjoying each moment
while they last.

THE END